A -Z

OF

EFFECTIVE

MINISTRY

Volume One

Tunde Jaiyebo

Published in Nigeria by

J-CHARIS Media House
Cultural Centre road, Mokola,
G. P. O. Box 15617 Dugbe,
Ibadan, Oyo State.

Tel: +234-8054582479
E-mail:chariscentraloffice@yahoo.com

CONTENTS

Ministry Is A Divine Trust

Ministry is God's channel for His servant to execute divine assignment on the earth. It is a divine trust. It is God entrusting His divine agenda, plan and purposes to man. Ministry, therefore, is a very serious issue which must be executed with every sense of responsibility. Ministry, being a divine trust must be carried out under the terms and conditions of the giver of the trust – God. Anything besides this would lead to a betrayal of divine trust.

Ministry is an honor bestowed on a man to carry out God's plan and purposes on the earth.

> *"...no man taketh this honour unto himself, but he that is called of God, as was Aaron."*

Hebrews 5:4.

Ministry is not done randomly. There must be a definite call to ministry and ministry must be executed as heaven expects.

This book is a simple guide to some basic principles needed to be effective in ministry.

CHAPTER A

Acknowledgement

The source, sustenance and success of ministry is based on an acknowledgement of God as the one who calls to and makes ministry effective. Ministry is a divine assignment and not a human vocation hence it must be undertaken with the consciousness of it being divine and carried out in line with divine instructions and guidelines. This is the key to longevity and effectiveness in ministry. Once a minister begins to arrogate to himself the success of his ministry, he gets disconnected to the source. In just a matter of time, his ministry would crumble.

The minister must understand that he is a minister (servant) of God and without God, he is nothing.

> *"Abide in me, and I in you. As the branch cannot bear fruit of itself, except it abide in the vine; no more can ye, except ye abide in me. I am the vine, ye are the branches: He that abideth in me, and I in him, the same*

bringeth forth much fruit: for without me ye can do nothing. If a man abide not in me, he is cast forth as a branch, and is withered; and men gather them, and cast them into the fire, and they are burned". **John 15:4-6.**

The minister must understand that God is his only source and He is indispensable. The God factor must be what the minister cannot do without. This fact must be constantly acknowledged by the minister.

"But by the grace of God I am what I am: and his grace which was bestowed upon me was not in vain; but I laboured more abundantly than they all: yet not I, but the grace of God which was with me". **1 Corinthians 15:10.**

There is no room for self in ministry – it must be God all the way.

"Not that we are sufficient of ourselves to think anything as of ourselves; but our sufficiency is of God; Who also hath made us able ministers of the new testament; not of the letter, but of the spirit: for the letter killeth, but the spirit giveth life". **2 Corinthians 3:5-6.**

The minister's source of strength must be in God.

"I can do all things through Christ which strengtheneth me". **Philippians 4:13.**

Failure to acknowledge God in ministry will lead to pride and pride always precedes a fall. A minister must never be maneuvered by the accolades of men to think he is a "self-made" man. He must acknowledge God and always give Him the glory. No man is allowed to tamper with or receive God's glory. Any attempt at such ultimately leads to destruction.

"And upon a set day Herod, arrayed in royal apparel, sat upon his throne, and made an oration unto them. And the people gave a shout, saying, it is the voice of a god, and not of a man. And immediately the angel of the Lord smote him, because he gave not God the glory: and he was eaten of worms, and gave up the ghost". **Acts 12:21-23.**

The uniqueness of ministry is rooted in the fact that ministry is not a natural assignment but a divine one. This means that the minister must constantly be connected to the Lord and regularly acknowledge Him in all.

"Ye have not chosen me, but I have chosen you, and ordained you, that ye should go and bring forth fruit, and that your fruit should remain: that whatsoever ye shall ask of the Father in my name, he may give it you".
John 15:16.

The minister must accept the fact that ministry is a divine responsibility. It is God entrusting man to carry out a divine assignment. This acknowledgement will naturally lead the minister to take necessary action with the right motive.

ACTION

Ministry is a divine assignment and must be undertaken with every sense of responsibility. The word "ministry" means area of service where a minister serves and "minister" means servant. Ministry is not a stroll in the park.

"This is a true saying, if a man desires the office of a bishop, he desireth a good work."
1 Timothy 3:1.

Being in ministry demands more than a desire. The desire must be expressed by accepting the work of ministry. No man is called into ministry by mere desire- it is a call of grace. Grace, however, is not a license to laziness. A minister must labour in the grace he has been called to.

> *"But by the grace of God I am what I am: and his grace which was bestowed upon me was not in vain; but I laboured more abundantly than they all: yet not I, but the grace of God which was with me."* **1 Corinthians 15:10**.

It is important for a minister to discover the area of service God has assigned him to function and serve. You cannot be an effective minister without serving in your allotted area of service. Every area of service is meant to serve specific groups of people – ministry is about the people. Without the discovery and acceptance of the area of service and the people to be served, ministry will not only be burdensome but also ineffective.

Paul the apostle was one of the most hardworking and apparently the most effective of all the apostles in the New Testament and he is worthy of our emulation. Paul not only knew what he was to do in ministry, but also those he was to serve in ministry.

> *"Whereunto I am appointed a preacher, and an apostle, and a teacher of the Gentiles".* **2 Timothy 1:11.**

He gave his all to the assignment and God backed him up withresults.

> *"But on the contrary, when they [really] saw that I had been entrusted [to carry] the Gospel to the uncircumcised [Gentiles, just as definitely] as Peter had been entrusted [to proclaim] the Gospel to the circumcised [Jews, they were agreeable]; For He Who motivated and fitted Peter and worked effectively through him for the mission to the circumcised, motivated and fitted me and worked through me also for [the mission to] the Gentiles. And when they knew (perceived, recognized, understood, and acknowledged) the grace (God's unmerited favor and spiritual blessing) that had been bestowed upon me, James and Cephas (Peter) and John, who were reputed to be pillars of the Jerusalem church, gave to me*

*and Barnabas the right hand of fellowship,
with the understanding that we should go to
the Gentiles and they to the circumcised
(Jews)* **Galatians 2:7-9. (Amplified).**

Here we also see that Peter was entrusted to have a ministry to the uncircumcised- the Jews. Faithfulness demands that the minister must work within the scope of his allotted sphere of influence. Pursuing and engaging in actions out of your "allotted ministry scope" is engaging in work that will not be rewarded.

Paul, however, had an uncanny desire and passion to minister outside the direct scope of his ordained ministry influence and each time he did that, he ran into a brick wall incurring pain, suffering and loss in the process.

Meaningful action that will be recognized by the master must revolve round the works expected to be done after the discovery of ministry assignment and those to be served. Once a man discovers his call to ministry, he must engage in intelligent action. The first action is to get prepared and equipped for the task ahead. Once God gives a go ahead, he must ensure that he puts in his all to execute the ministry. Ministry should never be done without adequate preparation.

There are three levels to executing ministry and all these are important to ensure that he does not make a shipwreck of his ministry:

1.   Call to ministry.

2.   Preparation to execute the call.

3.   Execution of the call.

These three stages are necessary actions to be taken by the minister (the first level of call to ministry is an act of God but the minister must respond to the call).

> *"PAUL, AN apostle–[special messenger appointed and commissioned and sent out] not from [any body of] men nor by or through any man, but by and through Jesus Christ (the Messiah) and God the Father, Who raised Him from among the dead."*
> **Galatians 1.1 (Amplified).**

Moses tried to jump the gun by trying to skip the preparation stage and consequently, he was sent to the desert for one-third of his life.

> *"And Moses was learned in all the wisdom of the Egyptians, and was mighty in words and in deeds. And when he was full forty years*

old, it came into his heart to visit his brethren the children of Israel. And seeing one of them suffer wrong, he defended him, and avenged him that was oppressed, and smote the Egyptian: For he supposed his brethren would have understood how that God by his hand would deliver them: but they understood not. And the next day he shewed himself unto them as they strove, and would have set them at one again, saying, Sirs, ye are brethren; why do ye wrong one to another? But he that did his neighbour wrong thrust him away, saying, Who made thee a ruler and a judge over us? Wilt thou kill me, as thou diddest the Egyptian yesterday? Then fled Moses at this saying, and was a stranger in the land of Madian, where he begat two sons". **Acts 7:22-29.**

Lack of preparation and inadequate preparation hinders ministry. Moses was "learned in all the wisdom of the Egyptians, and was mighty in words and in deeds" and he knew he had a call on his life.

> *"For he supposed his brethren would have understood how that God by his hand would deliver them: but they understood not".* **Acts 7:25.**

However, his natural training was not enough to empower him to execute the ministry God had for him. There was absolutely no way Moses would deliver Israel from the bondage of Egypt by mere physical one-on-one combat. The assignment needed spiritual strength and resources in which his natural training and qualification was deficient.

A minister must engage in the action of adequate training and preparation before venturing into ministry. Let us look at this point from the life of Paul.

> *"But when it pleased God, who separated me from my mother's womb, and called me by his grace, To reveal his Son in me, that I might preach him among the heathen; immediately I conferred not with flesh and blood: Neither went I up to Jerusalem to them which were apostles before me; but I went into Arabia, and returned again unto Damascus. Then after three years I went up to Jerusalem to see Peter, and abode with*

him fifteen days. But other of the apostles saw I none, save James the Lord's brother. Now the things which I write unto you, behold, before God, I lie not. Afterwards I came into the regions of Syria and Cilicia; And was unknown by face unto the churches of Judaea which were in Christ: But they had heard only, That he which persecuted us in times past now preacheth the faith which once he destroyed".

Galatians 1:15-23.

From this passage we see,

1. The call to ministry is an act of grace **(vs. 15).**

2. Paul's call to ministry was specifically to "the heathen" **(vs. 16).**

3. He took time to prepare **(vs. 16-19).**

The Lord Jesus Christ also engaged in the act of preparation before ministry. Apart from His brief encounter in Jerusalem at the age of twelve, He was not engaged in ministry until He was thirty.

"Now when all the people were baptized, it came to pass, that Jesus also being baptized,

and praying, the heaven was opened, And the Holy Ghost descended in a bodily shape like a dove upon him, and a voice came from heaven, which said, Thou art my beloved Son; in thee I am well pleased. And Jesus himself began to be about thirty years of age, being (as was supposed) the son of Joseph, which was the son of Heli". **Luke 3:21-23**.

Our Lord and Savior engaged in the act of preparation, and so must his ministers. It is commonly said that Jesus spent thirty years preparing for a ministry of three and a half years. This shows the importance of preparation. This generation, however, suffers from inadequate preparation which is the bane of ministry today. The quality of preparation will determine the quality of manifestation.

Another example of a minister who engaged in preparation was John the Baptist.

"And you, little one, shall be called a prophet of the Most High; for you shall go on before the face of the Lord to make ready His ways, to bring and give the knowledge of salvation to His people in the forgiveness and remission of their sins. Because of and

through the heart of tender mercy and loving-kindness of our God, a Light from on high will dawn upon us and visit [us] to shine upon and give light to those who sit in darkness and in the shadow of death, to direct and guide our feet in a straight line into the way of peace. And the little boy grew and became strong in spirit; and he was in the deserts (wilderness) until the day of his appearing to Israel [the commencement of his public ministry]".**Luke 1:76-80 Amplified.**

It must be emphasized that preparation for ministry is not a one- off event but a lifestyle. In ministry, the act of preparation is on- going. Preparation as a lifestyle releases the ability needed for the ministry.

ABILITY

Ministry can only be successfully done with ability. Ability is having the means or skill to do something. The first and most important ability is divine ability. God will never call a man to do anything without providing the needed ability. Divine ability must, however, be channeled through human ability. God gives His ministers ability in different forms and the major means is through the provision of spiritual gifts. Spiritual gifts are divine channels through which ability is produced. Spiritual gifts can be likened to the engine that powers ministry. Ministry can never be executed without the effective utilization of gifts. Every minister is endowed with the requisite gifts needed to get the job done. Spiritual gifts can therefore, be divided into two categories:

1.   **The gifts of the Holy Spirit:** These gifts are divine tools that produce divine ability to the minister in order to do ministry supernaturally. The gifts of the Holy Spirit are, however, "as the Spirit wills". They are only manifest at the behest, initiative and discretion of the Holy Spirit and not the minister.

> *"But all these worketh that one and the self-same Spirit, dividing to every man severally as he will"*. **1 Corinthians 12:1.**

One of the ministries of the Holy Spirit is to help the believer and this is the reason why He manifests His gifts through them so as to enable them to do ministry effectively. An evangelist, for example, will have the Holy Spirit manifest "the power gift" through him to be effective in his evangelistic ministry. These power gifts are working of miracles, gifts of healings and gifts of faith.

The Holy Spirit will manifest through a prophet the gift of "utterance and revelation gifts" These include prophecy, diverse kinds of tongues, interpretation of tongues, the words of wisdom, the words of knowledge and discerning of spirits.

A minister must desire to be used by the Holy Spirit to manifest the gifts of the Holy Spirit. The manifestation of the gifts of the Spirit provides supernatural ability to the minister to be effective in ministry.

2. **The Spiritual gifts of the minister:** The second category of the spiritual gifts which provides ability to the minister are the spiritual gifts God has sovereignly given to each minister to use to do ministry. Unlike the gift of the Holy Spirit, these gifts are given to the minister to use as "he wills". The use of these gifts provides the ability for effective ministry and it is the responsibility of every minister not only to discover the gifts in his

possession, but also to develop and maximally deploy them to execute his ministry.

"As every man hath received the gift, even so minister the same one to another, as good stewards of the manifold grace of God. If any man speak, let him speak as the oracles of God; if any man minister, let him do it as of the ability which God giveth: that God in all things may be glorified through Jesus Christ, to whom be praise and dominion forever and ever. Amen". **1 Peter 4:10-11.** Spiritual gifts are indispensable tools to ministry.

"Having then gifts differing according to the grace that is given to us, whether prophecy, let us prophesy according to the proportion of faith; Or ministry, let us wait on our ministering: or he that teacheth, on teaching; Or he that exhorteth, on exhortation: he that giveth, let him do it with simplicity; he that ruleth, with diligence; he that sheweth mercy, with cheerfulness". **Romans 12:6-8.**

Another source of ability the ministers must take advantage of are talents. Talents are God-given natural ability to do certain things well with ease. Every human being has been graciously talented by God and a minister must not undermine this as talents are sources of ability.

ANOINTING

It is absolutely impossible to do ministry effectively without the anointing. Anointing is divine enablement. Ministry is a divine assignment that can only be done by divine enablement- the anointing. An attempt at doing ministry without the anointing is a license to frustration and ineffectiveness. The anointing is always on a man for service.

> *"The Spirit of the Lord is upon me, because he hath anointed me to preach the gospel to the poor; he hath sent me to heal the brokenhearted, to preach deliverance to the captives, and recovering of sight to the blind, to set at liberty them that are bruised,"* **Luke4:18.**

When God anoints, He empowers for service.

"How God anointed Jesus of Nazareth with the Holy Ghost and with power: who went about doing good, and healing all that were oppressed of the devil; for God was with him." **Acts 10:38.**

The anointing is also the yoke-destroying, burden-removing power of God which is a critical tool needed in ministry.

"It shall come to pass in that day that his burden will be taken away from your shoulder and his yoke from your neck, and the yoke will be destroyed because of the anointing oil". **Isaiah 10:27.**

The devil, his operations and influences in the lives of people and in society can only be effectively neutralized and destroyed by the anointing. A minister without the anointing is no threat to the devil and his ministry will have little or no impact. The anointing is the power of God.

When God calls a man, He anoints the man to get the job done. Every gift comes with an anointing. Each of the five fold ministry gifts/offices come with the required anointing. A man who stands and operates in his ministry allows the anointing to show up and consequently, the manifestation of that gift. It is crucial for the anointing to be enhanced and channeled in the right direction.

How to enhance the anointing,

1.   Holy living.

2.   Prayer especially in tongues.

3.   Operating by and in faith when doing ministry.

4.   Dependence on the Holy Spirit.

5.   Prompt obedience to the Holy Spirit.

6.   Staying in the Word of God.

ACCESSIBILITY

A minister must be accessible in two major dimensions. He must be accessible to God and to the people. Ministry is divine assignment and being accessible to God is an indispensable ingredient to doing ministry effectively. A minister must be accessible to God in prayer and through God's Word.

As it is commonly said, a minister must not get so busy with the work of God that he ignores the God of the work.

Personal fellowship with God is sine qua non to the ministry that will be acceptable before God. A minister must be careful not to jeopardize his relationship with God in a bid to execute his ministry. He must be accessible to God and God must be accessible to him. The minister must understand his most vital responsibilities are prayer and a vibrant relationship with the Word of God – every other thing hinges on the success of these two things. Prayer and the Word are critical ways for the minister to have access to God. A minister who gets enmeshed in "delegatable" duties will dissipate his anointing and eventually render his ministry impotent. In the early church, the apostles understood this point. They understood that their core ministry was prayer and the word and other things were to be delegated.

> *"And in those days, when the number of the disciples was multiplied, there arose a murmuring of the Grecians against the Hebrews, because their widows were neglected in the daily ministration. Then the twelve called the multitude of the disciples*

unto them, and said, it is not reason that we should leave the word of God, and serve tables. Wherefore, brethren, look ye out among you seven men of honest report, full of the Holy Ghost and wisdom, whom we may appoint over this business. But we will give ourselves continually to prayer, and to the ministry of the word. And the saying pleased the whole multitude: and they chose Stephen, a man full of faith and of the Holy Ghost, and Philip, and Prochorus, and Nicanor, and Timon, and Parmenas, and Nicolas a proselyte of Antioch: Whom they set before the apostles: and when they had prayed, they laid their hands on them". **Acts 6:1-6**.

The consequence of the apostles giving time to prayer and the word was evident -

"And the word of God increased; and the number of the disciples multiplied in Jerusalem greatly; and a great company of the priests were obedient to the faith". **Acts 6:7.**

A minister's access to God by the minister results in effective ministry. The secret ministry of the minister in accessing God leads to the minister's success in the open. Time to relate, talk to and fellowship with God must never be toiled with. A minister must also develop his access to the Holy Spirit. He cannot go far without access to the ministry of the Holy Spirit. The Holy Spirit is "the advantage" of the believer.

Access to the Holy Spirit brings the following advantages:

1.   Guidance.

2.   Revelation of the future.

3.   Access to divine communication.

4. Access to power

> *"Howbeit when he, the Spirit of truth, is come, he will guide you into all truth: for he shall not speak of himself; but whatsoever he shall hear, that shall he speak: and he will shew you things to come"*. **John 16:13.**

Also, access to the Holy Spirit exposes and allows the believer to enjoy the gifts of the Holy Spirit.

> *But the manifestation of the Spirit is given to every man to profit withal. For to one is given by the Spirit the word of wisdom; to another the word of knowledge by the same Spirit; To another faith by the same Spirit; to another the gifts of healing by the same Spirit; To another the working of miracles; to another prophecy; to another discerning of spirits; to another divers kinds of tongues; to another the interpretation of tongues: But all these worketh that one and the selfsame Spirit, dividing to every man severally as he will".* **1 Corinthians 12:7.**

Accessibility to the minister also includes having access to quality people who can facilitate the success of his ministry.

> *"He that walketh with wise men shall be wise: but a companion of fools shall be destroyed".* **Proverbs 13:20.**

The minister must make himself accessible to the right kind of people.

> *"That ye be not slothful, but followers of them who through faith and patience inherit the promises".* **Hebrew 6:12.**

The second part of accessibility is the minister's accessibility to the people to which he is sent. Ministry is people- a minister must therefore make himself accessible to people. A minister must understand that his accessibility to God will determine the quality and effectiveness of his accessibility to people. Ministry can be burdensome, and it sometimes comes with crisis, pain, loss, discouragement etc. and at such low moments in the minister's life, he must understand his right of unfettered and unrestricted access to God to receive help.

> *"Seeing then that we have a great high priest, that is passed into the heavens, Jesus the Son of God, let us hold fast our profession. For we have not an high priest which cannot be touched with the feeling of our infirmities; but was in all points tempted like as we are, yet without sin. Let us therefore come boldly unto the throne of grace, that we may obtain mercy, and find grace to help in time of need".* **Hebrew 4:14-16.**

> *"Blessed be God, even the Father of our Lord Jesus Christ, the Father of mercies, and the God of all comfort; Who comforteth*

us in all our tribulation, that we may be able to comfort them which are in any trouble, by the comfort wherewith we ourselves are comforted of God". **2 Corinthians 1:3-4.**

This shows that ministry could hit the minister at the wrong end. At times like this, access to the comfort of God iscritical.

"For, when we were come into Macedonia, our flesh had no rest, but we were troubled on every side; without were fightings, within were fears. Nevertheless God, that comforteth those that are cast down, comforted us by the coming of Titus; And not by his coming only, but by the consolation wherewith he was comforted in you, when he told us your earnest desire, your mourning, your fervent mind toward me; so that I rejoiced the more" **2 Corinthians 7:5-7.**

God is primarily concerned about the minister's relationship with Him more than the work. As believers, we have been given access to the father and we must maximize this privilege.

"For through him we both have access by one Spirit unto the Father".

Ephesians 2:18.

CHAPTER B

Bible

The bible is the foundation and manual for ministry. Anything done in ministry outside of the spirit of the bible is totally unacceptable. A minister must have a working knowledge of the Bible. A minister cannot afford to be a biblical illiterate. A minister who does not have a working knowledge of the Bible is unknowingly courting shame.

> *"Study to shew thyself approved unto God, a workman that needeth not to be ashamed, rightly dividing the word of truth"*.

2 Timothy 2:15.

The Bible is central to effective ministry. In these days when the world view is warped, the minister must be grounded in the Bible else, he will be swept off his feet and become a proponent and advocate of demonic activities.

"I marvel that you are turning away so soon from Him who called you in the grace of Christ, to a different gospel, which is not another; but there are some who trouble you and want to pervert the gospel of Christ. But even if we, or an angel from heaven, preach any other gospel to you than what we have preached to you, let him be accursed". **Galatians 1:6-9.**

The behavior and practices of a minister must be based on the principles of the Bible. The Bible is the infallible Word of God and an indispensable tool for successful ministry. *"Every part of Scripture is God-breathed and useful one way or another--showing us truth, exposing our rebellion, correcting our mistakes, training us to live God's way. Through the Word we are put together and shaped up for the tasks God has for us"* **2 Timothy 3:16-17 (Message).**

The minister must recognize the value of the Bible – the Word of God.

1. It is the sword of the Spirit.

"And take the helmet of salvation, and the sword of the Spirit, which is the word of God;" **Ephesians 6:17**.

2. It is a hammer.

> *""Is not My word like a fire?" says the LORD, "And like a hammer that breaks the rock in pieces?"* **Jeremiah 23:29.**

3. It is fire.

> *""Is not My word like a fire?" says the LORD, "And like a hammer that breaks the rock in pieces"* **Jeremiah 23:29.**

4. It is alive and powerful.

> *"For the Word that God speaks is alive and full of power [making it active, operative, energizing, and effective];"* **Hebrew 4:12a. Amplified.**

5. It is a discerner of thoughts, intents and purpose.

> *"For the word of God is quick, and powerful, and sharper than any twoedged sword, piercing even to the dividing asunder of soul and spirit, and of the joints and marrow, and is a discerner of the thoughts and intents of the heart"*. **Hebrew 4:12. Amplified.**

6. It is purposeful, effective and target oriented.

> *"So shall my word be that goeth forth out of my*

mouth: it shall not return unto me void, but it shall accomplish that which I please, and it shall prosper in the thing whereto I sent it"*. **Isaiah 55:11.**

7. It illuminates.

"Thy word is a lamp unto my feet, and a light unto my path. **Psalms 119:105.**

8. It is reliable.

"For ever, O LORD, thy word is settled in heaven. **Psalms 119:89.**

9. It is seed.

"Now the parable is this: The seed is the word of God". **Luke 8:11.**

10. It is enduring.

"For all flesh (mankind) is like grass, and all its glory (honor) like [the] flower of grass. The grass withers and the flower drops off, But the Word of the Lord (divine instruction, the Gospel) endures forever. And this Word is the good news which was preached to you". **1 Peter 1:24-25, Amplified.**

11. It grows.

   "So mightily grew the word of God and prevailed". **Acts 19:20.**

12. It produces faith.

   "So then faith cometh by hearing, and hearing by the word of God". **Romans 10:17.**

BOLDNESS

Boldness means courage, confidence, fearlessness, frankness, valiance and plainness.

A minister is God's representative and boldness is required in carrying out his task because he is bound to face opposition in various forms. The minister is a target of the antics of the devil and boldness is a prerequisite for the minister to get the job done.

   "For yourselves, brethren, know our entrance in unto you, that it was not in vain: But even after that we had suffered before, and were shamefully entreated, as ye know, at Philippi, we were bold in our God to speak unto you the gospel of God with much contention". **1 Thessalonians 2:1-2.**

Areas where a minister must be bold;

1. Speech:

   "Great is my boldness of speech toward you, great is my glorying of you: I am filled with comfort, I am exceeding joyful in all our tribulation". **2 Corinthians 7:4.**

   "But even after that we had suffered before, and were shamefully entreated, as ye know, at Philippi, we were bold in our God to speak unto you the gospel of God with much contention". **1 Thessalonians 2:2**

2. Prayer:

   "Let us therefore come boldly unto the throne of grace, that we may obtain mercy, and find grace to help in time of need". **Hebrews 4:16**

How to develop boldness

1. Intimate fellowship with God in prayer and the Word:

   Fellowship provides intimacy which in turn provides accuracy and boldness.

"Now when they saw the boldness of Peter and John, and perceived that they were unlearned and ignorant men, they marvelled; and they took knowledge of them, that they had been with Jesus". **Acts 4:13**

2.   A conscious knowledge of who the minister represents.

3.   An awareness of the abiding presence of the Lord.

"Let your conversation be without covetousness; and be content with such things as ye have: for he hath said, I will never leave thee, nor forsake thee. So that we may boldly say, The Lord is my helper, and I will not fear what man shall do unto me". **Hebrew 13:5-6.**

4.   Prayer:

"Praying always with all prayer and supplication in the Spirit, and watching thereunto with all perseverance and supplication for all saints, And for me, that utterance may be given unto me, that I may open my mouth boldly, to make known the mystery of the gospel, For which I am an ambassador in bonds: that therein I may speak boldly, as I ought to speak". **Ephesians 6:18-20.**

"And now, Lord, behold their threatenings: and grant unto thy servants, that with all boldness they may speak thy word, By stretching forth thine hand to heal; and that signs and wonders may be done by the name of thy holy child Jesus. And when they had prayed, the place was shaken where they were assembled together; and they were all filled with the Holy Ghost, and they spake the word of God with boldness".

5. Not succumbing to fear:

    "For God hath not given us the spirit of fear; but of power, and of love, and of a sound mind". **2 Timothy 1:7.**

6. The understanding that he is answerable to God.

    "For do I now persuade men, or God? or do I seek to please men? for if I yet pleased men, I should not be the servant of Christ". **Galatians 1:10.**

7. Overcome the fear of making mistakes. A minister must understand that his self-esteem or acceptance by God is not based on performance but on relationship. The fear of mistakes could make a minister shrink back

from doing what ought to be done. He must understand that the most important thing is his relationship with God and God's help is available when mistakes occur or when the going gets tough.

"Seeing then that we have a great high priest, that is passed into the heavens, Jesus the Son of God, let us hold fast our profession. For we have not an high priest which cannot be touched with the feeling of our infirmities; but was in all points tempted like as we are, yet without sin. Let us therefore come boldly unto the throne of grace, that we may obtain mercy, and find grace to help in time of need". **Hebrew 4:14-16.**

Fear and ministry do not mix. Fear must be eliminated and replaced with boldness. Paul understood this; hence his admonition to Timothy

"Wherefore I put thee in remembrance that thou stir up the gift of God, which is in thee by the putting on of my hands. For God hath not given us the spirit of fear; but of power, and of love, and of a sound mind".

2 Timothy 1:6-7.

Timothy had issues with fear and intimidation. He was a gifted minister and Paul knew he had to step out in boldness. Fear and intimidation will dissipate the minister's ability to utilize his gifts. The minister must heed Paul's admonition to Timothy to deploy God's resources (power, love, sound mind) to overcome fear and step out in boldness to make full proof of ministry.

The minister must be bold - doing the right thing at the right time in the right way regardless of how he feels or the opposition he faces.

BACKBONE

> *"Looking unto Jesus the author and finisher of our faith; who for the joy that was set before him endured the cross, despising the shame, and is set down at the right hand of the throne of God."* **Hebrew 12:2.**

To make any appreciable impact in the ministry, a minister must be able to endure hardship. He must be resilient and resolute. A person who cannot persevere will never amount to much in life. Nothing comes easy in life – a price has to be paid to get anything worthwhile done. When the going gets tough, the minister must buckle up and stick to his God-given dream, he must understand that patience is a virtue which he cannot afford to neglect. Patience is doing the same thing without wavering. It is enduring pain, suffering or inconvenience until we achieve a desired result. It is having a backbone. Paul admonished Timothy to develop backbone,

> *"Thou therefore, my son, be strong in the grace that is in Christ Jesus. And the things that thou hast heard of me among many witnesses, the same commit thou to faithful men, who shall be able to teach others also. Thou therefore endure hardness, as a good soldier of Jesus Christ".* **2 Timothy 2:3.**

The minister must be strong in the grace available in Christ. There is a strength that only comes from our union with Christ.

Ministry is not always a smooth road. There will be times of difficulty and at such times, the minister must have the backbone to weather the storm.

"Thou therefore endure hardness, as a good soldier of Jesus Christ". **2 Timothy 2:3.**

The Lord Jesus Christ had backbone and gave a model for ministers to follow.

> *"Looking unto Jesus the author and finisher of our faith; who for the joy that as set before him endured the cross, despising the shame, and is set down at theright hand of the throne of God".* **Hebrews 12:2.**

He had enough backbone to despise the shame. Two critical things are important from Jesus' examples for the minister who will develop backbone. The Lord Jesus went through and endured physical pain. The cross was the most painful death to go through. Ministry will involve enduring physical pain and ministers must have the backbone not to be limited by it.

> *"But in all things approving ourselves as the ministers of God, in muchpatience, in afflictions, in necessities, in distresses, In stripes, in imprisonments, in tumults, in labours, in watchings, infastings".*

2 Corinthians 6:4-5.

"Are they ministers of Christ? (I speak as a fool) I am more; in labours more abundant,

in stripes above measure, in prisons more frequent, in deaths oft. Of the Jews five times received I forty stripes save one. Thrice was I beaten with rods, once was I stoned, thrice I suffered shipwreck, a night and a day I have been in the deep; In journeyings often, in perils of waters, in perils of robbers, in perils by mine own countrymen, in perils by the heathen, in perils in the city, in perils in the wilderness, in perils in the sea, in perils among false brethren; In weariness and painfulness, in watchings often, in hunger and thirst, in fastings often, in cold and nakedness".

2 Corinthians 11:23-27.

The minister must be physically strong. Ministry is demanding and it is important that the minister must be healthy. He must keep fit physically else, the demands of ministry might crush him.

The second dimension of the endurance of Jesus was emotional. Jesus despised the shame. **Hebrew 12:2.** The death on the cross was the most shameful death anyone could have experienced. It was the death reserved for the worst of criminals. Jesus, though innocent, went through this kind of death. Despite this, He had the backbone to survive. The minister must be emotionally strong to handle the vicissitudes that come with ministry.

> *"In weariness and painfulness, in watchings often, in hunger and thirst, in fastings often, in cold and nakedness. Beside those things that are without, that which cometh upon me daily, the care of all the churches".*

2 Corinthians 11:27-28.

Many times, ministry comes with emotional stress. There will be times of disappointment and betrayal. Sometimes, the investment of time, money and effort seems to have gone down the drain. At times like this, a minister must be emotionally strong.

CHAPTER C

Character

A minister, being a servant of God also represents God. He must therefore exhibit godly character. This will usually be evident in crisis.

"Then came the children of Israel, even the whole congregation, into the desert of Zin in the first month: and the people abode in Kadesh; and Miriam died there, and was buried there. And there was no water for the congregation: and they gathered themselves together against Moses and against Aaron. And the people chode with Moses, and spake, saying, Would God that we had died when our brethren died before the LORD! And why have ye brought up t he congregation of the LORD into this wilderness, that we and our cattle should die there? And wherefore have ye made us to come up out of Egypt, to bring us in unto this

evil place? it is no place of seed, or of figs, or of vines, or of pomegranates; neither is there any water to drink. And Moses and Aaron went from the presence of the assembly unto the door of the tabernacle of the congregation, and they fell upon their faces: and the glory of the LORD appeared unto them. And the LORD spake unto Moses, saying, Take the rod, and gather thou the assembly together, thou, and Aaron thy brother, and speak ye unto the rock before their eyes; and it shall give forth his water, and thou shalt bring forth to them water out of the rock: so thou shalt give the congregation and their beasts drink. And Moses took the rod from before the LORD, as he commanded him.And Moses and Aaron gathered the congregation together before the rock, and he said unto them, Hear now, ye rebels; must we fetch you water out of this rock?

And Moses lifted up his hand, and with his rod he smote the rock twice: and the water came out abundantly, and the congregation drank, and their beasts also. And the LORD spake unto Moses and Aaron, Because ye believed me not, to sanctify me in the eyes of the children of Israel, therefore ye shall not bring this congregation into the land which I have given them. " **Numbers 20:1-12.**

There was a crisis and there was no water not even for animals. verse 2-5.

Water is an essential commodity to human sustenance and in this situation, it was a critical issue because the children of Israel were in the desert.

Lack of water caused disaffection, dissatisfaction and disenchantment. There was a problem. The lives of people and cattle were in danger. Moses rose to the occasion and made the competent use of his gift and office to solve the problem.

Moses knew what to do at this time of crisis. He consulted God and solved the problem.

"And Moses and Aaron went from the presence of the assembly unto the door of the tabernacle of the congregation, and they fell upon their faces: and the glory of the LORD appeared unto them. And the LORD spake unto Moses, saying, Take the rod, and gather thou the assembly together, thou, and Aaron

thy brother, and speak ye unto the rock before their eyes; and it shall give forth his water, and thou shalt bring forth to them water out of the rock: so thou shalt give the congregation and their beasts drink. And Moses took the rod from before the LORD, as he commanded him." **Numbers 20:6-9.**

"And Moses lifted up his hand, and with his rod he smote the rock twice: and the water came out abundantly, and the congregation drank, and their beasts also." Verse 11.

His competence solved the crisis and he became a hero before the people. As far as they were concerned at that time, Moses was simply awesome. The application of competence to resolve crisis exposes and elevates the competent person to an enviable position. Moses was indeed a competent leader.

But beloved not every act of competence is acceptable before God.

"And the LORD spake unto Moses and Aaron, Because ye believed me not, to sanctify me in the eyes of the children of Israel, therefore ye shall not bring this congregation into the land which I have given them." **Numbers 20:12.**

Not every heroic act of competence is pleasing to God. King Saul won the battle against the Amalakites - brought spoils of war, paraded Agag the captured king but God rejected him.

"And Saul smote the Amalekites from Havilah until thou comest to Shur, that is over against Egypt. And he took Agag the king of the Amalekites alive, and utterly destroyed all the people with the edge of the sword. But Saul and the people spared Agag, and the best of the sheep, and of the oxen, and of the fatlings, and the lambs, and all that was good, and would not utterly destroy them: but everything that was vile and refuse, that they destroyed utterly. Then came the word of the LORD unto Samuel, saying, It repenteth me that I have set up Saul to be king: for he is turned back from following m e , a n d h a t h n o t p e r f o r m e d m y commandments. And it grieved Samuel; and he cried unto the LORD all night."

Samuel 15:7-11.

Jesus said in **Matthew 7:22-23** *"Many will say to me in that day, Lord, Lord have we not* *prophesied in thy name? and in thy name have cast out devils? And in thy name done many wonderful works? And then will I profess unto them, I never knew thee, depart from me that work iniquity"*

When God sees through the minister's competence, he must also see good character. A minister must never be double-faced. Competent without character presents unacceptable results to God which leads to the termination of such a ministry. This was the case of Moses which was quite pathetic and we must learn from his mistake.

"Now all these things happened unto them for ensamples: and they are written for our admonition, upon whom the ends of the world are come. Wherefore let him that thinketh he standeth take heed lest he fall. There hath no temptation taken you but such as is common to man: but God is faithful, who will not suffer you to be tempted above that ye are able; but will with the temptation also make a way to escape, that ye may be able to bear it." **1 Corinthians 10:11-13.**

The curriculum vitae of Moses was very impressive:

- Led over two million out of Egypt, the land of bondage.

- He dealt with Pharaoh, the most powerful king of that time.

- He was a prophet, judge and administrator.

At every crisis, his competence was always seen. This includes parting the Red sea, providing meat and water when there was none in the wilderness.

> *"And Moses was an hundred and twenty years old when he died: his eye was not dim, nor his natural force abated. And the children of Israel wept for Moses in the plains of Moab thirty days: so the days of weeping and mourning for Moses were ended. And Joshua the son of Nun was full of the spirit of wisdom; for Moses had laid his hands upon him: and the children of Israel hearkened unto him, and did as the LORD commanded Moses."*

Deuteronomy 34:7-10.

Moses died at the age of one hundred and twenty and was described as the meekest man on earth.

> *"(Now the man Moses was very meek, above all the men which were upon the face of the earth.)"* **Numbers 12:3.**

He also had the following strengths and features:

His eyesight was still sharp.

His body was still strong.

His eyes were not dim nor his natural force abated

He spoke face to face with God.

He performed great miracles, signs and wonders even in his old age.

He wrote the first 5 books of the Bible.

It is unimaginable that someone like this would have any character flaws. Yet, Moses, despite his status and achievement, had anger management problems. He even saw God's handwriting but because of his character flaw, he broke the tablets upon which God's handwriting was inscribed. He also destroyed the golden calf, ground it and mixed it with water and made the people drink it.

"And Moses turned, and went down from the mount, and the two tables of the testimony were in his hand: the tables were written on both their sides; on the one side and on the other were they written. And the tables were the work of God, and the writing was the writing of God, graven upon the tables. And when Joshua heard the noise of the people as they shouted, he said unto Moses, There is a noise of war in the camp. And he said, It is not the voice of them that shout for mastery, neither is it the voice of them that cry for being overcome: but the noise of them that sing do I hear. And it came to pass, as soon as he came nigh unto the camp, that he saw the calf, and the dancing: and Moses' anger waxed hot, and he cast the tables out of his hands, and brake them beneath the mount. And he took the calf which they had made, and burnt it in the fire, and ground it to powder, and strawed it upon the water, and made the children of Israel drink of it." **Exodus 32:15-20**.

How do you develop character?

A Christian's character profile should be characterized by the fruit of the Spirit. This means that what he needs to do is to yield to the Holy Spirit.

> *The fruit of the Spirit is love, joy, peace, longsuffering, gentleness, goodness, faith, Meekness, temperance: against such there is no law."* **Galatians 5:22-23.**

Confessing God's word will also help a minister to build his character. Your confession is what eventually becomes your reality.

> *"This book of the law shall not depart out of thy mouth; but thou shalt meditate therein day and night, that thou mayest observe to do according to all that is written therein: for then thou shalt make thy way prosperous, and then thou shalt have good success."* **Joshua 1:8.**

Character will blossom when one engages in prompt repentance, prompt adjustment and prompt obedience.

It is pertinent to do a self-analysis and provide honest answers to these questions,

- Are you a man/woman of character?

- Can we really see God's nature in you?

- Do you have a character flaw?

- Are you proud, touchy, and prone to anger?

- When God looks beyond your competence, does He see good character?

A minister must understand the place of discipline. Discipline is key to success.

"Do you not know that in a race all the runners compete, but [only] one receives the prize? So run [your race] that you may lay hold [of the prize] and make it yours. Now every athlete who goes into training conducts himself temperately and restricts himself in all things. They do it to win a wreath that will soon wither, but we [do it to receive a crown of eternal blessedness] that cannot wither. Therefore I do not run uncertainly (without definite aim). I do not box like one beating the air and striking without an adversary. But [like a boxer] I buffet my body [handle it roughly, discipline it by hardships] and subdue it, for fear that after proclaiming to

others the Gospel and things pertaining to it, I myself should become unfit [not stand the test, be unapproved and rejected as a counterfeit]".

1 Corinthians 9:24-27 (AMPLIFIED)

CALLING

Ministry is a response to the call of God. It is God that calls to ministry. The call of God is a divine summon to an office, task or responsibility. You cannot do ministry independent of God's call. Ministry must never be undertaken as a human responsibility or a result of human or self-appointment.

"From Paul, an apostle, not by human appointment or human commission, but by commission from Jesus Christ and from God the Father who raised him from the dead" **Galatians 1:1. New English Bible.**

A man must never assume or arrogate God's call to himself. This is a wrong reason to be in ministry. Other wrong reasons are:

a. A perceived qualification: Graduation from a Bible school is not evidence of being called into ministry. Training will only assist a called man and it never authenticates the uncalled into ministry.

b. Perceived spirituality or maturity: This does not necessarily mean such a person must do ministry.

c. Human judgement: Sometimes people might pressurize a seemingly serious and dedicated Christian to step out into a ministry into which he has not been called.

d. Human compensation and reward: Ministry must never be a reward of compensation for dedication and loyalty but the result of a definite call by God.

e. Human arrangement in pursuit of career or profession: Ministry must be a response to the call of God. The five fold ministry is the result of Christ Himself setting aside men and making them ministry gifts to the body.

> *"(Now that he ascended, what is it but that he also descended first into the lower parts of the earth? He that descended is the same also that ascended up far above all heavens, that he might fill all things.) And*

he gave some, apostles; and some, prophets; and some, evangelists; and some, pastors and teachers" **Ephesians 4:9-11.**

A minister is a "called" man- a man set apart for a divine assignment. It is an act of grace – not due to merit, qualification or works.

When a man is called, he must respond, prepare and get equipped to execute the call. The call determines the parameters and boundaries of ministry. A minister who dabbles into a calling that is not his will not only dissipate his anointing but also, stands the risk of losinghis ministry.

The call of God should be what determines a minister's focus.

"For Christ sent me not to baptize, but to preach the gospel: not with wisdom of words, lest the cross of Christ should be made of none effect." **1 Corinthians 1:17.**

The definite call of God is what gives the minister conviction to execute ministry at all cost.

CONVICTION

Conviction is an indispensable ingredient to carry on in ministry. While conviction does not guarantee success in ministry, the absence of conviction is simply a license to failure. There are many components that will make a leader successful but one of the most critical is conviction.

Conviction is an absolute belief and deep persuasion that something is right, and must be done. Conviction is what you stand for and what you aim to achieve. Conviction is having an inescapable drive to get something done because you are persuaded that is what ought to be done. Conviction is what fuels the burning desire of a minister to plunge on in ministry against all odds. Conviction creates a sense of necessity. Conviction is what powers drive and consistency in ministry.

> *"For though I preach the gospel, I have nothing to glory of: for necessity is laid upon me; yea, woe is unto me, if I preach not the gospel!"* **1 Corinthians 9:16.**

The minister must be a person on a mission who is convinced beyond all doubt that his mission is possible. He must know that he is under a heavenly mandate to do ministry. Conviction is the staying power that sustains ministry. Without conviction, the minister will cave in at the pressures that ministry faces. Conviction is not fleshly determination but a divine staying power emanating from the call of God. Many ministers have abandoned their call due to the vicissitudes of life and the onslaught of the evil one.

COMMUNICATION

Human beings are classified as social beings. We need meaningful relationships to thrive and survive. There can be no meaningful relationship without meaningful communication. Communication is important in ministry as ministry involves dealing with and relating with people. Every great relationship is rooted in effective communication. Communication is a skill that every minister must acquire and effectively deploy in the execution of his ministry. The role of authentic, clear and effective communication cannot be overemphasized. Poor communication will hinder ministry. A minister who cannot effectively communicate will be an ineffective minister, irrespective of the other qualities that he possesses. Communication might not have direct bearing on the minister's anointing but it could limit the scope of influence of the minister's anointing.

Critical Channels Of Communication In Ministry

1. Preaching and teaching

2. One on one communication

3. Communicating to and with a group

4. Internet and social media communication

5. Writing and publishing (books, tracts, magazines, letters etc.)

6. Singing, praise and worship

7. Evangelism

8. Television and radio

Components Of Effective Communication

"Now, brethren, if I come to you speaking in [unknown] tongues, how shall I make it to your advantage unless I speak to you either in revelation (disclosure of God's will to man) in knowledge or in prophecy or in

instruction? If even inanimate musical instruments, such as the flute or the harp, do not give distinct notes, how will anyone [listening] know or understand what is played? And if the war bugle gives an uncertain (indistinct) call, who will prepare for battle? Just so it is with you; if you in the [unknown] tongue speak words that are not intelligible, how will anyone understand what you are saying? For you will be talking into empty space! There are, I suppose, all these many [to us unknown] tongues in the world [somewhere], and none is destitute of [its own power of] expression and meaning. But if I do not know the force and significance of the speech (language), I shall seem to be a foreigner to the one who speaks [to me], and the speaker who addresses [me] will seem a foreigner to me". **1 Corinthians 14:6-11. Amplified.**

1. Have a specific, clear intended purpose

2. Effective transmission of intended purpose to your audience

3.   Reception of your intended purpose by your audience

4.   Processing by your audience

5.   Action by your audience in the way you intended.

Communication is a skill that must be acquired by the minister. A minister's communication must be:

- Clear and unambiguous

- Easily understood

- Precise

- Accurate

- Compelling

- Motivational

CHAPTER D

Diligence

It takes a minister who is faithful to his call to be diligent. The way a minister applies due diligence to the gifts and grace of his life and ministry determines the extent to which he fulfills his ministry.

Understanding your call and ministry will only be translated into meaningful and worthwhile activities that will bless people if there is a diligent application of the resources and opportunities that God brings your way as a minister. Ministry is work and diligence is what powers work to be translated into results.

Diligence is a steady effort. It is careful hard work. It is also the painstaking attention and care legally required of someone. Diligence is intelligent hard work that produces the desired result.

Diligence means doing the right thing regularly in the right way without interruption. Diligence means steady effort. It is devoid of every form of inconsistency and impersistence. When the minister's effort is sporadic, irregular and inconsistent, he is not diligent. The truth of the matter is this: a man who does not put in steady effort in the execution of his assignment cannot be trusted with anything. Inconsistency isunfaithfulness.

> *"Confidence in an unfaithful man in the time of troubles is like a broken tooth and a foot out of joint."* **Proverbs 25:19.**

More Scriptures On Diligence

Proverbs 10:4 *" He becometh poor that dealeth with a slack hand: but the hand of the diligent maketh rich."*

Proverbs 12: 24, 27 *"The hand of the diligent shall bear rule: but the slothful shall be under tribute"*

Vs 27" The slothful man roasted not that which he took in hunting: but the substance of a diligent man is precious"

Proverbs 22:29 *"seeth thou a man diligent in his business? He shall stand before kings; he shall not stand before mean men"*

Proverbs 27:23 *"Be thou diligent to know the state of thou flocks, and look well to thou herds"*

2 Corinthians 8:22 *" And we have sent with them our brother, whom we have oftentimes proved diligent in many things but now much more diligent upon the great confidence which I have in you".*

Hebrew 11:6 *"But without faith it is impossible to please Him for he that cometh to God must believe that he is and the rewarded them that diligently seek Him.*

DECORUM

Ministry is a high calling and decorum is expected. Decorum deals with ethics, etiquette and protocols.

Ethics – "The moral principles that govern a person's behavior of the conducting of an activity". Oxford Dictionary.

Etiquette – "The customary code of polite behavior in society or among the members of a particular profession or group". Oxford Dictionary

Protocol – "The accepted or established code of procedure or behavior in any group, organization or situation"Oxford Dictionary.

We will look at the three dimensions together and refer to them simply as decorum.

The person and personality of the minister

1. Appearance: Appearance must reflect the office/status becoming of a minister. The minister represents God and His people, hence, his appearance must never be unbecoming.

   "For the LORD seeth not as man seeth; for man looketh on the outward appearance, but the LORD looketh on the heart". **1 Samuel 16:7b.**

2. Association: A minister must never associate with people or groups of questionable character.

   "Be not deceived: evil communications corrupt good manners." **1 Corinthians 15:33.**

3. Reputation: He must be highly spoken of. His reputation must be above board.

   "Receive us; we have wronged no man, we have corrupted no man, we have defrauded no man". **2 Corinthians 7:2.**

A minister must consciously build and protect his reputation.

"Also, people outside the church must speak well of him so that he will not be disgraced and fall into the devil's trap." **1 Timothy 3:7 New Living Translation.**

"I will no longer talk much with you, for the ruler of this world is coming, and he has nothing in Me." **John 14:3**

4. Lifestyle:

    a. Not extravagant

    b. Law- abiding

    c. Promise keeper

    d. Good demeanour i.e. good reputation

Money Matters

1. A minister must be discreet in handling money. He must have the right attitude towards money.

    "Not given to wine, no striker, not greedy of filthy lucre; but patient, not a brawler, not covetous" **1Timothy 3:3.**

"Feed the flock of God which is among you, taking the oversight thereof, not by constraint, but willingly; not for filthy lucre, but of a ready mind;" **1 Peter 5:2.**

A minister must avoid two dangerous mentalities about money.

A. Scarcity/shortage mentality: Money is a critical tool in ministry and a minister's attitude and handling of it is very important. A minister must avoid having a wrong financial mindset.

He must understand that there is no shortage in the world, only artificial scarcity to benefit a few and their interest. The devil wants to deny ministry of funds but the minister must never have a shortage or scarcity mentality.

"The profit of the earth is for all; the king himself is served by the field" **Ecclesiastes 5:9.**

Scarcity/shortage mentality is reflected in:

(i) A continuous discontent

-    No matter how much you have, it is never enough

-    You don't enjoy life and what you have because

you think there isn't enough for you and the prospect of getting more is very slim.

"But godliness with contentment is great gain". **1 Timothy 6:6.**

A minister must be content – making use of available resources and trusting God to supply his needs.

> *Not that I speak in respect of want: for I have learned, in whatsoever state I am, therewith to be content. I know both how to be abased, and I know how to abound: every where and in all things I am instructed both to be full and to be hungry, both to abound and to suffer need. I can do all things through Christ which s t rengtheneth me".* ***Philippians 4:11-13.***

(ii) Selfishness, stinginess and over possessiveness: They believe that they do not have enough to share hence, the greedy desire to accumulate things because there isn't enough for everybody. They think that giving is losing and diminishing their scarce resources and therefore, give little or nothing at all. They cut themselves off from the spiritual dimension of money making.

*"Give, and it shall be given unto you; good measure, pressed down, and shaken together, and running over, shall men give into your bosom. For with the same measure that ye mete withal it shall be measured to you again". **Luke 6:38.***

"But this I say, He which soweth sparingly shall reap also sparingly; and he which soweth bountifully shall reap also bountifully". **2 Corinthians 9:6**

(iii) Resentment against those who have what they seek to be theirs.

\- You cannot have what you despise.

(iv) Unthankful for what they have because they think they deserve more but don't have more.

The minister must also avoid:

B. Poverty mentality- an attitude of helplessness that renders a person incapable of maximizing his potential.

Characteristics of poverty mentality

(i) A Mindset that blinds a person from recognizing his ability to change his circumstances.

(ii) Undue dependence on others (government, church, friends etc.) for help. Such people think that they need direct help or input from others. - They think and act stuck and helpless.

(iii) Abdicates responsibility for their lives situation and circumstances: -If he is not helped, then he is helpless and it's not his fault.

- They expect people to do for them what they ought to dothemselves

(iv) He has little or no appreciation for his/her potential.

- He belittles and underestimate his ability and resources

- He suffers a low self-esteem

(v) Complacency: Too comfortable in his comfort to take bold step to cause changes

(vi) Unproductive: not using what you have to get the desired results. Being ungrateful for where you are and what you have, but moaning over where you are not and what you don't have.

A minister must destroy these mindsets through prayer and renewing the mind.

The minister's work

Decorum is also essential in carrying out the minister's work. He must be characterized with:

1. Confidentiality

2. Diligence

3. Excellence

4. Promptness

Opposite Sex

Decorum is very critical in sexual matters as it is one area that the devil tries to truncate many destinies.

> *"For by means of a whorish woman a man is brought to a piece of bread: and the adulteress will hunt for the precious life."* **Proverbs 6:26.**

"But whoso committeth adultery with a woman lacketh understanding: he that doeth it destroyeth his own soul. A wound and dishonour shall he get; and his reproach shall not be wiped away. For jealousy is the rage of a man: therefore he will not spare in the day of vengeance. He will not regard any ransom; neither will he rest content, though thou givest many gifts". **Proverbs 6"32-35.**

Here are some guidelines in relating with the opposite sex:

1. Never visit opposite sex alone

2. Avoid emotional dependence by opposite sex

3. Honour the married

4. Never sleep (have sexual relations) with anybody asides your spouse.

Pulpit

The pulpit is a sacred place and decorum is needed. A minister who is ministering on another minister's pulpit should bear these issues in mind:

1. Always acknowledge the host when he is invited as guest minister.

2. Never make policy issues on another minister's pulpit.

3. Never preach doctrine contrary to host or make host look incompetent.

4. Always keep to time.

5. Observe the title of host.

6. Never raise money for yourself on another minister's pulpit.

7. Never discuss host with members.

8. After ministration, contact host to thank him for opportunity to minister.

CHAPTER E

Example

A minister must be an example. His life must be worthy of emulation. He must exemplify Christ and the Christian life. One of the qualifications of a leader, which a minister is, is that he must have a good report.

> *"Moreover he must have a good report of them which are without"* **1Timothy 3:7a.**

> *"Outsiders must think well of him"* **1Timothy 3:7a. Message**

> *"Also, people outside the church must speak well of him"* **1Timothy 3:7a. New Living Translation**

> *"People who are not Christians must speak well of him,"* **1Timothy 3:7a. God's Word**

"Neither as being lords over God's heritage, but being ensamples to the flock." **1 Peter 5:3.**

"Let no man despise thy youth; but be thou an example of the believers, in word, in conversation, in charity, in spirit, in faith, in purity." **1Timothy 4:12.**

A minister must be "followable". He must not just preach but be a model.

"For our gospel came not unto you in word only, but also in power, and in the Holy Ghost, and in much assurance; as ye know what manner of men we were among you for your sake." **1Thessalonians 1:5-7.**

A minister worth his salt will challenge his people to follow his example.

"For yourselves know how ye ought to follow us: for we behaved not ourselves disorderly among you; Neither did we eat any man's bread for nought; but wrought with labour and travail night and day, that we might not be chargeable to any of you: Not because we have not power, but to make ourselves an ensample unto you to follow us." **2 Thessalonians 3:7-9.**

"Brethren, be followers together of me, and mark them which walk so as ye have us for an ensample. " **Philippians 3:17.**

EXPERIENCE

A minister is a leader and a leader should not be a novice. A novice is a person new or inexperienced in a field. A novice is a beginner or new convert.

"Not a novice, lest being lifted up with pride he fall into the condemnation of the devil". **1 Timothy 3:6.**

A minister must be spiritually mature. He must have some clear-cut experience in the things of God. The call to ministry is a high calling and it is not to be ventured into by new converts.

The role of apprenticeship and mentorship is indispensable in the formation of a minister. Formal education like Bible school is good but nothing can take the place of practical hands-on training under a seasoned minister. Exigency must be acquired on handling people as ministry deals mainly with people. Inexperience in handling and dealing with people can ruin ministry. Experience must also be acquired in financial matters. It is also important to be skilled and experienced in handling the word of God.

… *"study to shew thyself approved unto god, a workman that needeth not to be ashamed, rightly dividing the word of truth "* **2 Timothy 2:15.**

Experience in the things of God has nothing to do with age but with the depth of spiritual influence which a minister has yielded. This is what guides his conduct and lifestyle.

EXCELLENCE

A minister must exemplify God's quality of excellence. God is excellent.

1.   His Name is excellent **Psalm 8:1, 9**

2.   His greatness is excellent **Psalm 150:2**

3.   He does excellent things **Isaiah 12:5**

4.   He is excellent in working **Isaiah 28:29**

5.   The Name of Jesus is excellent **Hebrews 1:4**

6. The ministry of Jesus is excellent **Hebrews 8:6**

7. His loving-kindness is excellent **Psalm 36:7**

Mediocrity does not glorify God. A minister must be excellent.

What is excellence?

- Surpassing the set standard

- Quality of being extremely very good

- Admirable, exceptional, superb, first class

- Being a model and a reference point

- Being above board before God and man (meet divine and human standards).

A good bible definition of excellence is found in **Daniel 6:1-6**

> **Verse 4 (New Living Translation)** *"Then the other administrators and high officers began searching for some fault in the way Daniel was handling government affairs, but they couldn't find anything to criticize or condemn. He was faithful, always responsible, and completely trustworthy."*

Excellence demands that under scrutiny, the minister's work:

1)   Cannot be faulted - "We don't give people any opportunity to find fault with how we serve."

2)   Is done faithfully - **1 Corinthians 4:1-2** *"Let a man so account of us, as of the ministers of Christ, and stewards of the mysteries of God. Moreover it is required in stewards, that a man be found faithful."*

3)   Is done honestly – right motive even when there is error, it is an honest mistake – a justifiable slip or error.

4)   Is done without mistakes – God is perfect and a minister must strive with the help of the Holy Spirit to attain perfection and be without any mistakes. It is important that if however mistakes occur, a minister should never excuse his mistakes. He must rather admit, repent, take correction and move on.

Excellence is dynamic – so a minister must aspire to do better today what he did yesterday. He must improve per time and every time. Yesterday's excellence is today's mediocrity.

Areas of Ministry Excellence

a) The minister himself – his person/personality: - excellence starts with the minister as a person before it shows up in his work.

Personal spiritual life: A minister must have a vibrant spiritual life. He must not be so consumed with the work of God that he ignores the God of the work.

- Personal fellowship is crucial to sustain and walk in excellence in ministry. A vibrant personal relationship with God produces intimacy which leads to precision and accuracy at all times. **Isaiah 48:17, Psalm 32:8-9, John 16:13**.

A minister's work is spiritual work and spiritual accuracy is critical. A minister's personal walk with God is the bedrock of excellence in ministry.

It is important for the minister to acquire certain skills to promote his excellence:

"He chose David also his servant, and took him from the sheepfolds: From following the ewes great with young he brought him to feed Jacob his people, and Israel his inheritance. So he fed them according to the integrity of his heart; and guided them by the skilfulness of his hands". **Psalms 78:70-72.**

He must acquire skills in:

- Discipline – demands training drills, routine and regiment. **1 Corinthians 9:24-27.**

- Punctuality – time management

- Focusing

- Lifestyle – money, friends, relationship with the opposite sex

- Speech – **Colossians 4:6**

- Emotion – anger, moodiness

Appearance: Leadership is image. You represent God and His people so appear accordingly:

Watch your dressing:

+ avoid attire of a harlot

+ avoid bad colour combination

+ appear as formal as possible and look presentable every time.

(b) Quality of leadership (accurate, relevant and impactful)

Excellence should be a lifestyle and an attitude and not an event.

Enemies of excellent leadership

A minister must watch out for these dangers that can destroy excellence:

1) Inconsistency: *"Unstable as water, thou shalt not excel;"* **Genesis 49:4**.

Inconsistency denies you:

- A track record of success

\- Ability to be a reference point

It portrays unreliability which destroys trust and influence (the bedrock of leadership).

2) Comparison and competitive jealousy:

> *"For we dare not make ourselves of the number, or compare ourselves with some that commend themselves: but they measuring themselves by themselves, and comparing themselves among themselves, are not wise."*
> **2 Corinthians 10.12**

Comparison and competitive jealousy will lead to -

\- Distraction

\- Break of focus

\- Diversion of energy, resources and anointing

\- Making the minister the second best – a duplicate of another.

3) Inadequate training/qualification.

4) Inadequate resources and adverse environment (know the resources

you need and trust God to supply).

5)   Laziness - not being inclined to work.

-       Not translating and developing your leadership from basic rudimentary level to higher quality which can be preserved or reach a larger scope.

"The slothful man roasteth not that which he took in hunting: but the substance of a diligent man is precious." **Proverbs 12.27**

6)   Faulty self-esteem.

7)   Lack of vision and clear sense of direction.

"Where there is no vision, the people perish". **Proverbs. 29:18.A**

8)   Burn-out: Avoid exhaustion and burn out as much as possible. Take a rest if you must but ensure that there is no vacuum created as a result of your absence. You should consult a senior pastor to make proper arrangements while you are away.

Tips for excellent leadership

1.   Vision and a clear sense of direction.

-    Doing the right thing at the right time with the correct motive.

-    The more you stay with your vision the better you become at it.

2.   Be an expert.

3.   Develop confidence in your God-given ability **1 Peter. 4:10, 1 Corinthians 3:10, Romans 12:6.**

-    You are appointed, gifted and you have the grace to lead so walk consciously in this reality.

4.   Effective team **Ecclesiastes 4:9-10.**

5.   A set of standard and appropriate strategies **Luke 14:28-32.**

6.   A review/assessment mechanism: even God had some time to review his work. God "saw that every stage of creation was good".

7.   Prayer. Intimacy breeds accuracy and produces

spiritual power and enablement.

8. Total dependence on God **Philippians 4:13.**

9. Continuous growth and learning **Proverbs. 18:15 New Living Translation** *"Intelligent people are always ready to learn. Their ears are open for knowledge."*

10. Diligence **Proverbs 22:29; 1 Corinthians. 4:1-2.**

11. Strategic relationships: "iron sharpens iron" **Acts 18:24-28.**

12. Go for Obedience to your call and to divine instructions as these will be the basis of your rewards by the master. **2 Corinthians 5:9-10.**

Other books from J-CHARIS Media House

- YOUR LIFE COUNTS
- THANK GOD YESTERDAY ENDED LAST
  NIGHT
- A FOOL'S PROFILE
- LAZY BONES AND WHAT THEY DO
- PROUD PEOPLE AND WHAT THEY DO
- ANGRY PEOPLE AND WHAT THEY DO
- USE IT OR MISS IT
- THANK GOD FOR POTIPHAR'S WIFE
- INTIMATE EXPRESSIONS
- WORRY
- GUILT
- FORGIVENESS 101
- HELP! MY PRAYERS ARE NOT WORKING
- NO WAY, MR DEVIL
- REJECTION
- OFFENCE
- THE POWER OF THE SEED
- MOVING FORWARD THROUGH DILIGENCE
- EFFECTIVE LEADERSHIP
- A to Z OF EFFECTIVE MINISTRY